SMART MONEY MOVES

A Guide for Teens and Young Adults

Kuphrey Eshiet

ISBN-13: 9798884687332
ISBN-10: 1477123456

Cover design by: Art Painter
Library of Congress Control Number: 2018675309
Printed in the United States of America

To the resilient spirits of youth, whose curiosity and determination shape the future. May this guide serve as a compass on your journey towards financial empowerment and independence. Your potential knows no bounds, and with smart money moves, may you navigate the seas of opportunity with confidence and wisdom.

CONTENTS

INTRODUCTION

Welcome to "Smart Money Moves: A Guide for Teens and Young Adults." In a world where financial literacy is essential for navigating the complexities of modern life, this book serves as your compass, guiding you towards a future of financial independence and success.

As teenagers and young adults, you stand at the threshold of a world filled with possibilities, opportunities, and challenges. From managing your first paycheck to planning for long-term financial goals, the decisions you make today will profoundly impact your future.

But the path to financial freedom can often seem daunting. With so much information available, it's easy to feel overwhelmed and unsure of where to begin. That's where this guide comes in. "Smart Money Moves" is designed to provide you with the knowledge, skills, and confidence you need to navigate the world of personal finance with ease.

Throughout the pages of this book, you'll find practical advice, actionable strategies, and real-life examples to help you make smart financial decisions. Whether you're learning how to create a budget, save for college, or invest in your future, each chapter is packed with valuable insights to help you build a strong financial foundation.

But this book is more than just a guide to managing money, it's a roadmap to financial empowerment. By mastering the principles of financial literacy, you'll gain greater control over your life, more opportunities for success, and the freedom to pursue your dreams on your own terms.

So, are you ready to take control of your financial future? Let's embark on this journey together and discover the power of "Smart Money Moves."

PREFACE

Welcome to "Smart Money Moves: A Guide for Teens and Young Adults." In a world where financial literacy is paramount to success, this book stands as a beacon, guiding you through the intricate landscape of personal finance.

As teenagers and young adults, you're embarking on a journey filled with endless possibilities and exciting opportunities. However, navigating the realm of money management can often feel like traversing uncharted territory. From budgeting to investing, from saving to spending wisely, the decisions you make today will shape your financial future.

This guide is designed to demystify the complexities of finance and empower you to make informed choices. Whether you're just starting your first job, considering higher education, or dreaming of entrepreneurial ventures, the principles outlined within these pages will provide you with the tools and knowledge to take control of your financial destiny.

Throughout this book, you'll discover practical tips, real-life examples, and actionable strategies to help you build a solid foundation for financial success. But beyond mere financial gain, this journey is also about cultivating a mindset of responsibility, resilience, and resourcefulness.

As you embark on this transformative journey, remember that every step you take towards financial literacy is a step towards greater freedom and autonomy. Embrace the challenges, seize the opportunities, and let "Smart Money Moves" be your trusted companion on the road to financial empowerment.

Here's to your journey towards a brighter, more prosperous future. Let's embark together.

CHAPTER 1:
MONEY BASICS

Money—it's a fundamental aspect of our lives, yet many of us feel overwhelmed or uncertain when it comes to managing it effectively. In this chapter, we'll lay the groundwork for your financial journey by exploring the basic principles of money management.

Understanding Income and Expenses

At its core, personal finance is all about balance. Balancing what you earn (income) with what you spend (expenses). Understanding your income and expenses is the first step towards achieving financial stability.

Budgeting Effectively

Budgeting is the cornerstone of financial management. It involves creating a plan for allocating your income to cover your expenses, savings, and financial goals. By budgeting effectively, you gain control over your money and ensure that you're living within your means.

To create a budget, start by listing all your sources of income, including wages, allowances, and any other money you receive regularly. Next, track your expenses by categorizing them into essentials (such as housing, food, and transportation) and non-essentials (such as entertainment and dining out). Compare your income to your expenses to see where your money is going and identify areas where you can cut back or reallocate funds.

Tracking Your Spending

Tracking your spending is essential for staying on budget and identifying spending patterns. Keep a record of every purchase you make, whether it's through a smartphone app, spreadsheet, or notebook. Review your spending regularly to identify any areas where you're overspending or where you can make adjustments to align with your financial goals.

Differentiating Between Needs and Wants

One of the key principles of financial management is distinguishing between needs and wants. Needs such as food, shelter, and healthcare are essential for survival and well-being. Wants, on the other hand, are non-essential items or experiences that bring pleasure or convenience but are not necessary for survival, e.g. a brand-new watch, the latest gadget, etc.

Understanding the difference between needs and wants

is crucial for making informed spending decisions. By prioritizing your needs and being mindful of your wants, you can allocate your resources more effectively and avoid overspending.

In the next section, we'll explore banking essentials and the importance of establishing a solid financial foundation through banking.

Banking Essentials

Discover the importance of opening a bank account, understanding debit vs. credit cards, and harnessing the power of compound interest.

One of the foundational steps for teens and young adults in financial planning is establishing a strong relationship with banking institutions. Let's explore the significance of opening a bank account, understanding the differences between debit and credit cards, and harnessing the power of compound interest.

Importance of Opening a Bank Account

For our target audience of teens and young adults, opening a bank account is more than just a financial transaction —it's a critical step toward financial independence and responsibility. A bank account is a secure place to store your money, providing easy access for transactions while offering safeguards against loss or theft.

By opening a bank account, you gain access to essential financial services such as depositing checks, withdrawing cash, and managing your funds electronically through online banking platforms. Additionally, having a bank account enables you to build a relationship with a financial institution, which may offer opportunities for future financial products and services, such as loans or credit cards.

Understanding Debit vs. Credit Cards

In today's digital age, plastic cards have become ubiquitous tools for making purchases and managing finances. However, teens and young adults need to understand the key differences between debit and credit cards and use them wisely.

Debit Cards: A debit card is linked directly to your bank account, allowing you to spend only your available money. When you use a debit card, funds are immediately deducted from your account, making it a convenient and straightforward way to access your money. Debit cards are ideal for everyday purchases and ATM withdrawals, providing a convenient alternative to cash.

Credit Cards: Unlike debit cards, credit cards allow you to borrow money from the card issuer up to a certain limit. When you use a credit card, you're essentially taking out a short-term loan, which you're required to repay later. Credit cards offer benefits such as rewards programs, fraud protection, and the ability to build credit history. However, it's crucial to use credit cards responsibly and pay off your balance in full each month to avoid high-interest charges and debt accumulation.

Harnessing the Power of Compound Interest

Compound interest is a financial concept that has the potential to work wonders for your savings and investments over time. For our target audience of teens and young adults, understanding compound interest is like unlocking a secret weapon for building wealth.

Definition: Compound interest is the interest earned on both the initial principal and the accumulated interest from previous periods. In simple terms, it's interest on interest, resulting in exponential growth of your money over time.

Example: Let's say you deposit $1,000 into a savings account that earns an annual interest rate of 5%. At the end of the first year, you'll earn $50 in interest, bringing your total balance to $1,050. In the second year, you'll earn interest not only on your initial $1,000 but also on the $50 interest earned in the first year. This cycle continues, with your money growing exponentially over time.

Conclusion

For those embarking on their financial journey, opening a bank account, understanding the nuances of debit and credit cards, and harnessing the power of compound interest are foundational principles that pave the way for financial success. By mastering these concepts, you can build a solid financial foundation and make informed decisions that will serve you well throughout your life.

CHAPTER 2: SAVING AND INVESTING

The Magic of Saving

Saving is the cornerstone of financial stability and success. In this chapter, we'll delve into the transformative power of saving money and how it can pave the way for achieving your financial goals.

Benefits of Creating an Emergency Fund

An emergency fund is your financial safety net, providing peace of mind and protection against unexpected expenses or life events. Whether it's a medical emergency, a car repair, or a sudden job loss, having a dedicated emergency fund can help you weather financial storms without resorting to debt or derailing your long-term goals.

By setting aside a portion of your income in an emergency fund, you're investing in your future resilience and financial security. Aim to build an emergency fund that covers three to six months' worth of living expenses, ensuring you have enough to cover essential bills and obligations in times of need.

Saving for Short-Term Goals

While it's essential to plan for the future, don't overlook the importance of saving for short-term goals as well. Whether it's a vacation, a new laptop, or a down payment on a car, having specific short-term goals gives you something tangible to work towards and keeps you motivated on your saving journey.

When setting short-term goals, be specific, measurable, and realistic. Break down larger goals into smaller, manageable milestones, and celebrate your progress along the way. By prioritizing your short-term goals and setting aside money regularly, you'll be amazed at how quickly you can turn your dreams into reality.

Following the 50/30/20 Rule

The 50/30/20 rule is a simple yet powerful budgeting guideline that can help you allocate your income effectively and achieve a balanced financial life. According to this rule:

<u>50% of your income should go towards your needs</u>: This includes essential expenses such as housing, utilities, groceries, and transportation. By keeping your needs within this portion of your budget, you ensure that you're covering the essentials without overspending.

<u>30% of your income should go towards your wants</u>: This category encompasses discretionary expenses such as dining out, entertainment, and non-essential purchases. While it's important to enjoy life and treat yourself

occasionally, keeping your wants within this portion of your budget ensures that you're living within your means and prioritizing your financial goals.

20% of your income should go towards savings and investments: This portion of your budget is reserved for building your financial future. Whether it's contributing to retirement accounts, saving for emergencies, or investing in your education or career advancement, prioritizing savings and investments ensures that you're setting yourself up for long-term financial success.

Following the 50/30/20 rule helps you strike a balance between meeting your immediate needs, enjoying life's pleasures, and investing in your future. It's a flexible framework that can adapt to your changing financial circumstances and goals, providing a roadmap for financial stability and prosperity.

In the next section of this chapter, we'll explore the world of investing and how you can grow your wealth over time through smart investment strategies.

Investing 101

Investing is a powerful tool for building wealth over the long term and understanding the basics is essential for financial success. In this section, we'll explore key investment options, risk management strategies, and the importance of starting early.

Stocks, Bonds, and Mutual Funds

Stocks: When you buy a stock, you're purchasing a share of ownership in a company. Stocks offer the potential for high returns over time, but they also come with higher volatility and risk. Investing in individual stocks requires careful research and analysis to identify companies with strong growth potential and financial stability.

Bonds are debt securities that corporations, governments, or municipalities issue to raise money. When you buy a bond, you're essentially lending money to the issuer in exchange for regular interest payments and the return of your principal at maturity. Bonds are generally considered safer investments than stocks, offering predictable income and capital preservation.

Mutual Funds: Mutual funds pool money from multiple investors to invest in a diversified portfolio of stocks, bonds, or other assets. By investing in mutual funds, you gain access to professional management and diversification, making them a popular choice for investors seeking broad exposure to the market with less risk.

Risk Tolerance and Diversification

Understanding your risk tolerance is crucial for building a balanced investment portfolio that aligns with your financial goals and comfort level. Risk tolerance refers to your willingness and ability to withstand fluctuations in the value of your investments.

If you have a high-risk tolerance, you may be comfortable with greater volatility and the potential for higher returns, whereas if you have a low-risk tolerance, you may prefer more conservative investments with lower volatility and slower growth.

Diversification is a risk management strategy that involves spreading your investments across different asset classes, industries, and geographic regions to reduce the impact of any single investment's performance on your overall portfolio. By diversifying your investments, you can minimize risk and enhance long-term returns.

Starting Early: The Power of Compounding

One of the most powerful factors in investing is time. Starting early allows you to take advantage of the power of compounding, where your investment returns generate additional earnings, which in turn generate even more earnings over time.

By investing early and consistently, you give your money more time to grow, potentially multiplying your initial investment many times over. Even small contributions made regularly can snowball into significant wealth over the long term, thanks to the exponential growth of compound interest.

Conclusion

Investing in stocks, bonds, and mutual funds offers the potential for long-term wealth accumulation, but it's essential to understand the risks and benefits before diving in. By diversifying your investments, managing risk effectively, and starting early, you can set yourself up for financial success and achieve your long-term goals. In the next section, we'll explore strategies for managing debt and building a solid financial foundation.

CHAPTER 3:
HANDLING DEBT

In Chapter 3, we get into the important subject of debt management, looking at ways to comprehend student loans, stay out of the debt trap, and manage debt sensibly. Readers may manage the complexity of debt and attain long-term financial security by grasping these ideas.

Steer clear of the debt trap

Debt can be a double-edged sword: while it can present chances for investment and growth, it can also turn into a burden that impedes the advancement of one's finances. To achieve long-term financial stability, we'll examine methods in this chapter for avoiding the debt trap and managing debt sensibly.

Making Responsible Use of Credit Cards

When used sensibly, credit cards may be useful financial instruments that provide incentives, convenience, and security. To prevent getting sucked into a debt trap that is too big for you to handle, it is necessary to comprehend how credit cards operate.

Above all, to prevent interest and late fees, make sure you pay your credit card account in full and on time each month. To avoid going over budget and taking on debt, keep a close eye on your expenditures and stick to them.

Furthermore, pay attention to your credit usage ratio, which indicates how much of your available credit you are actually utilizing. To preserve your credit score and prevent adverse effects on your financial situation, try to keep your credit utilization percentage below 30%.

Understanding Student Debt

To pay for tuition, fees, and living expenses, a large number of young adults who want to pursue higher education frequently need to take out student loans. Even though taking out student loans might be a wise investment in your future, it's important to understand the conditions and ramifications of borrowing money for school.

Consider all of your possibilities for financial assistance, such as work-study, grants, and scholarships, before taking out student loans. Examine conditions, interest rates, and repayment alternatives carefully when comparing loan offers from various lenders.

After obtaining student loans, devise a repayment strategy that aligns with your financial objectives and budget. To reduce your monthly payments and expedite repayment, take into account choices like income-driven repayment programs, loan consolidation, or refinancing.

Prudent Debt Management

Whether you have school loans, credit card debt, or other types of debt, keeping your finances in good shape requires prudent debt management. To minimize interest costs and lower the total cost of borrowing, start by giving high-interest debt priority and making proactive payments on it.

To address several debts methodically, take into account techniques like the debt avalanche or debt snowball method. By paying off the lowest obligation first, you roll that payment over to the next smallest loan, and so on, using the debt snowball method. To reduce interest expenses over time, you can use the debt avalanche method to give priority to the loans with the highest interest rates.

To free up more money for debt repayment, look at ways to boost income and decrease expenses in addition to paying off debt. To hasten the payoff of your debt, make the required cutbacks, bargain with creditors for reduced interest rates or fees, and take into account alternate sources of income like a part-time job or freelancing.

You may steer clear of the debt trap and create the foundation for a better financial future by managing your debt sensibly, understanding student loans, and using credit cards carefully. In the following section of this chapter, we will examine credit reports and ratings as well as methods for establishing and preserving excellent credit.

Reports and Credit Scores

Your credit score is a critical component of your overall financial health since it affects your capacity to take out loans, obtain credit, and meet other financial objectives. This part will cover the significance of credit reports and ratings, as well as how to monitor your credit history, establish good credit, and correct credit errors.

Establishing Good Credit

Getting a house, getting a reasonable interest rate on a loan, and sometimes even getting a job all depend on having good credit. Numerous criteria, such as the duration of your credit history, the sorts of credit accounts you have, your payment history, credit use, and recent credit queries, all affect your credit score.

To establish good credit, focus on the following approaches:

Pay bills on time. Your payment history is the main factor in determining your credit score. Pay all of your bills on time each month, including your utilities, loans, and credit card bills.

Control credit utilization: To maintain a healthy credit utilization ratio, keep your credit card balances modest in comparison to your credit limits. Try to avoid having your utilization go below 30% since this will lower your credit score.

Create a varied combination of credit: Having a variety of credit accounts, such as retail, installment, and credit card accounts, can help you improve your credit score. But only create new accounts when necessary, and refrain from applying for several loans or credit cards at once.

Keeping an Eye on Your Credit History

It's critical to keep a regular eye on your credit history to spot fraud, identity theft, and mistakes. Every year, via AnnualCreditReport.com, you are entitled to a complimentary copy of your credit report from each of the three major credit bureaus: Equifax, Experian, and TransUnion.

Make sure to thoroughly check your credit reports for any errors, including missing accounts, inaccurate personal information, or evidence of fraudulent activity. To make sure your credit report is correct, raise any inaccuracies with the credit bureaus and the creditor providing the data.

Correcting Credit Errors

Take quick action to fix any inaccuracies you detect on your credit report. Send a written letter to the credit bureaus along with supporting proof for your dispute. Within a timeframe, the credit bureaus must look into your dispute and make any necessary corrections.

Be proactive in raising your credit score over time, in addition to challenging inaccuracies. Prioritize timely bill payments, minimize credit card debt, and refrain from obtaining additional credit inquiries unless absolutely required. You can progressively raise your credit score and reach your financial objectives with perseverance and sound financial practices.

By learning how to monitor your credit history, repair credit errors, and establish good credit, you can take charge of your financial destiny and open doors to favorable terms for credit and borrowing.

CHAPTER 4: GETTING A JOB AND MAKING MORE MONEY

We address the important subject of work and income growth in Chapter 4, with advice on how to choose a career route, manage education and skill development, and take advantage of networking opportunities. Readers can take charge of their career paths and realize their professional objectives by grasping these ideas.

Picking a Professional Route

Your career has a big impact on how much money you can make, how happy you are at work, and how much you can make altogether. We'll look at methods in this section for picking a vocation that fits your interests, abilities, and objectives.

Managing the Choice Between Emotion and Reality

Selecting a career path can be difficult, especially when you have to decide between pursuing your passion and being realistic. While it's important to pursue a career that excites you and fits with your interests, it's also important to take into account pragmatic aspects like market demand, wage potential, and employment availability.

Spend some time thinking about your values, interests, and

strengths as you explore this choice. Examine chances to integrate your hobbies with pragmatic issues and think about how your passions and skills fit with possible professional options. To discover the ideal fit for you, be open to exploring other fields and professions, and maintain an open mind.

Examine your education and skill development.

The improvement of one's skills and education is crucial for advancing one's profession. Investing in your education can enhance your earning potential and open doors to new opportunities, regardless of whether you're seeking self-directed study, vocational training, or a typical college degree.

Think about your professional objectives and look into school options that fit your dreams. Examine your alternatives for professional development courses, formal schooling, and certifications that can assist you in gaining the abilities and information required to be successful in your chosen industry.

Discover the Value of Networking

Building a professional network through networking can help you connect with other professionals, gain insight from their experiences, and discover undiscovered job prospects. Developing a strong professional network can help you discover mentors and advisers, learn more about your sector, and advance your career.

Utilize industry conferences, professional groups in your field, and networking events to expand your network. Actively seek out professionals in your field, both online and in person, and develop sincere connections founded on shared objectives and interests. Don't forget to add value to your network by helping people, sharing your knowledge, and being a trustworthy source.

In summary, selecting a career path is an important choice that can affect your general well-being and financial future. You can position yourself for success in your chosen area by learning how to balance practicality and enthusiasm, looking into chances for education and skill development, and realizing the value of networking. Throughout your work, keep in mind to be flexible, value lifelong learning, and actively seek out chances for development and progress.

CHAPTER 4: CAREER AND INCOME GROWTH

Negotiating Salaries and Benefits

Negotiating salaries and benefits is a crucial aspect of career development, enabling you to advocate for fair compensation, understand employee benefits, and plan for long-term career success. In this section, we'll explore strategies for effectively negotiating your salary and benefits package to ensure you're fairly compensated for your skills and contributions.

Advocate for Fair Compensation

Advocating for fair compensation begins with understanding your worth in the job market and articulating your value to potential employers. Research industry standards and salary ranges for your desired position, taking into account factors such as location, experience, and qualifications. Use online resources, salary surveys, and networking connections to gather information and benchmark your salary expectations.

During salary negotiations, be prepared to articulate your skills, accomplishments, and the value you bring to the organization. Emphasize tangible achievements, such as increased revenue, cost savings, or successful projects, to demonstrate your impact and justify your salary request. Be confident, assertive, and professional in your negotiations, and be willing to walk away if the offer does not meet your expectations.

Understand Employee Benefits

Besides salary, employee benefits play a significant role in your overall compensation package and can impact your financial well-being and quality of life. Take the time to understand the benefits offered by your employer, including health insurance, retirement plans, paid time off, and other perks.

Evaluate the value of each benefit and consider how it aligns with your needs and priorities. For example, a comprehensive health insurance plan with low premiums and extensive coverage may be more valuable to you than a higher salary with minimal benefits. Similarly, a generous retirement plan with employer-matching contributions can significantly enhance your long-term financial security.

Plan for Long-Term Career Success

Negotiating salaries and benefits is not just about short-term gains—it's also about positioning yourself for long-term career success and advancement. Consider the potential for growth and development within the organization, opportunities for skill enhancement and professional advancement, and the overall cultural fit and alignment with your career goals.

When evaluating job offers, look beyond the immediate compensation package and consider the broader implications for your career trajectory and personal fulfillment. Assess the company's reputation, stability, growth prospects, potential for career advancement, and opportunities for learning and development.

Conclusion

Negotiating salaries and benefits is essential for achieving fair compensation, maximizing your earning potential, and planning for long-term career success. By advocating for fair compensation, understanding employee benefits, and prioritizing opportunities for growth and advancement, you can set yourself up for a fulfilling and rewarding career journey.

CHAPTER 5: REAL-LIFE SCENARIOS

We'll examine actual situations that young adults could run across while navigating their financial journeys in this chapter. We'll talk about useful ways to make smart choices and get financially stable, from picking whether to rent or buy a home to getting ready for big events in your life like getting married and having kids.

Buying versus renting

Whether to buy or rent a house is one of the biggest financial decisions that young adults must make. We'll examine the benefits and drawbacks of each choice, taking into account elements like flexibility, affordability, and long-term investment potential. Readers can make decisions that are in line with their financial goals and personal preferences by thinking about these things and knowing what each choice means.

In this section, we'll explore the considerations of renting an apartment versus homeownership and provide insights into mortgage basics to help readers make informed decisions about their housing choices.

Considerations for Renting an Apartment

Renting an apartment offers flexibility and freedom, making it an attractive option for individuals who prioritize mobility and minimal commitment. Some key considerations for renting include

Flexibility: Renting allows for greater flexibility to move as needed, making it ideal for individuals who anticipate changes in their living situation or career.

Maintenance: The landlord or property management company typically takes care of property maintenance and repairs, so renters are not typically responsible for these duties.

Financial Considerations: Renting may require fewer upfront costs compared to homeownership, as renters typically only need to pay a security deposit and monthly rent.

Limited Control: Renters have limited control over the property, including restrictions on renovations, decor changes, and pet ownership, depending on the terms of the lease agreement.

A Look Into Home Ownership

Now let's go over important topics for anyone thinking about becoming a homeowner, like saving money for a down payment, figuring out the mortgage application process, and being aware of the continuous expenditures associated with owning a home, such as insurance, taxes, and maintenance fees. Readers can approach homeownership with confidence and financial readiness if they comprehend these variables and make plans appropriately.

Considerations of Homeownership

Homeownership offers stability, equity building, and the potential for long-term financial growth. However, it also comes with additional responsibilities and financial commitments. Some key considerations for homeownership include the following:

Equity Building: Homeownership allows individuals to build equity over time as they pay down their mortgage and property values appreciate.

Stability: Owning a home provides stability and a sense of permanence, making it an attractive option for individuals looking to put down roots in a community.

Tax Benefits: Homeowners may be eligible for tax deductions on mortgage interest, property taxes, and other homeownership-related expenses, providing potential financial benefits.

Maintenance and Responsibilities: Homeowners are responsible for property maintenance, repairs, and upkeep, which can entail additional time, effort, and costs.

Grasping Mortgage Basics

For those considering homeownership, understanding the basics of mortgages is essential. A mortgage is a type of loan used to finance the purchase of a home. Some key concepts to grasp include

Down Payment: The down payment is the initial upfront payment made towards the purchase price of the home. It is typically expressed as a percentage of the total purchase price.

Interest Rate: The interest rate is the cost of borrowing money and is expressed as a percentage of the loan amount. It can have a significant impact on the total cost of homeownership over the life of the loan.

Loan Term: The loan term is the length of time over which the mortgage is repaid. Common loan terms include 15-year and 30-year mortgages, each with its own advantages and considerations.

Monthly Payments: Mortgage payments typically consist of principal and interest, with additional amounts for property taxes, homeowner's insurance, and, if applicable, private mortgage insurance (PMI).

Understanding these mortgage basics can help individuals evaluate their borrowing options, compare loan offers from different lenders, and make informed decisions about homeownership.

Events in Life and Financial Readiness

Events in life like getting married, having children, or saving for retirement can have a big impact on finances. We'll talk about ways to be financially prepared, such as setting aside money for a wedding, estimating child-rearing expenditures, and investing for retirement. Through proactive planning and anticipating key life events, readers may reduce financial stress and confidently accomplish their long-term objectives.

Wills and Estate Planning

Even though estate planning is essential to financial planning, many people, especially young people, ignore it. We'll go over how important it is to make a will, name beneficiaries, and set up powers of attorney to honor your desires in case of death or incapacity. Readers can reduce taxes, safeguard their possessions, and ensure the financial security of their loved ones in the future by taking the time to draft an estate plan.

Insurance: Life, health, and auto insurance protect against unforeseen circumstances and monetary losses, making it a crucial part of financial planning. We'll go over the many insurance coverage options, such as life, health, and vehicle insurance, and how to choose the appropriate coverage amounts and policies for your particular needs. Readers may protect their financial well-being by making informed decisions and knowing how insurance works to mitigate risk and protect assets.

Conclusion

In summary, renting an apartment versus homeownership is a significant decision that involves various financial, lifestyle, and personal considerations. By understanding the pros and cons of each option and grasping the basics of mortgages, individuals can make informed decisions that align with their financial goals, preferences, and circumstances.

CHAPTER 6:
CREATING WEALTH

We explore wealth-building techniques in Chapter 6, emphasizing asset investments, passive income generation, and adhering to the FIRE movement's tenets. By putting these techniques into practice, readers can establish a life of prosperity and freedom, accelerate money-building, and become financially independent.

Growing your net worth

Investing sensibly, managing your money carefully, taking advantage of growth and passive income opportunities, and managing your finances strategically are all important components of building wealth. We'll look at ways to increase your net worth in this area, such as investing in assets, generating passive income, and exploring the Financial Independence, Retire Early (FIRE) movement.

Investing in Assets

Asset acquisition is a crucial part of creating long-term wealth. Whether you invest in stocks, bonds, real estate, or other alternative assets, you can grow your net worth and generate profits by allocating your capital wisely. Important asset-investing techniques include the following:

Diversification: Spreading out your investments by diversifying them helps you get the best returns and reduces risk. To lower the risk of concentrated exposure and promote resilience, consider distributing your investments throughout several asset classes, sectors, and geographical areas.

Long-Term Perspective: When investing long-term, you may use compounding to your advantage and weather market volatility. Avoid trying to time the market or chase short-term gains. Instead, build a diverse portfolio that matches your risk tolerance and financial goals.

Regular Contributions: Over time, investing accounts, like brokerage or retirement accounts, can amass wealth more quickly when contributions are made regularly. Set up automatic payments and use dollar-cost averaging to build your portfolio steadily and level out changes in the market.

How to generate Passive Income

Earned income can be supplemented or replaced by passive income, which is income produced with little continuous work or active involvement. Rental properties, dividend-paying equities, interest on bonds or savings accounts, and royalties from intellectual property are a few examples of typical passive income sources.

Building income-producing assets and investment vehicles that create cash flow without needing ongoing supervision or active management is the key to earning passive income. Think about investing in rental properties, peer-to-peer lending platforms, dividend reinvestment plans (DRIPs), or developing digital goods or online courses.

Exploring the FIRE Movement

The Financial Independence, Retire Early (FIRE) movement is a way of life and financial philosophy that emphasizes saving, investing wisely, and practicing frugal living to achieve early retirement. The goal of the FIRE movement is to amass enough money to support their lifestyle forever, freeing people up to pursue their hobbies and passions without having to have a regular job.

To adopt the FIRE movement's tenets, concentrate on cutting costs, raising savings rates, and refining investment plans to accelerate the accumulation of wealth. People can attain financial freedom and early retirement on their terms by leading a minimalist lifestyle, placing a higher value on money than material belongings, and developing other sources of income.

Contributing to Society

While accumulating wealth is crucial for safeguarding one's financial future, contributing to society's well-being and giving back to others are just as vital. This section will discuss the value of volunteering, making charitable contributions, and striking a balance between one's personal wealth and societal responsibilities.

The Value of Donating to Charity

Giving to charities is essential to helping groups and projects that deal with social, environmental, and humanitarian issues. Donating money, time, or resources to charitable causes allows people to positively impact their communities and the lives of others while also making a significant difference in the world.

Giving to charities promotes empathy, compassion, and a sense of purpose while also bringing about personal fulfillment and a sense of purpose. Contributing to charitable causes that are near and dear to one's heart, as well as local NGOs and international relief groups, enables people to leave a lasting legacy of love and generosity.

The Benefits of Volunteering

Apart from monetary contributions, volunteering is an additional effective means of giving back and changing the world. You can directly support charitable organizations' missions and contribute to the resolution of urgent social issues by giving your time, talents, and expertise to them.

Additionally, volunteering provides chances for skill development, networking, and personal development. Participating in volunteer work, whether it be at a food bank, animal shelter, or community center, enables people to make important connections with others and further the common good.

Juggling Social Responsibility and Personal Wealth

While building personal wealth is a noble endeavor, it's critical to strike a balance between achieving financial success and ethical and social duty. Rich people have privilege and power, and they must use their resources for the common good and to help create a society that is more just and equal.

Developing a stewardship and giving mentality, putting other people's welfare first, and taking the bigger picture into account while making financial decisions are all necessary to strike a balance between personal prosperity and social responsibility. This could be promoting environmental sustainability, helping socially conscious companies, or actively participating in campaigns to solve structural problems like injustice, inequality, and poverty.

Contributing to society is not only a moral duty but also a necessary component of creating a purposeful and happy existence. Individuals can leave a legacy of compassion, generosity, and social change by accepting the value of volunteering, giving charity, and striking a balance between personal wealth and societal responsibility.

In essence, building wealth is not just about accumulating financial assets—it's about creating a life of abundance, freedom, and fulfillment while making a positive impact on the world around you. By adopting a holistic approach to wealth-building that encompasses strategic investing, passive income generation, embracing financial independence, and giving back to others, individuals can achieve true prosperity and create a legacy of lasting significance.

Conclusion

Throughout "Smart Money Moves: A Guide for Teens and Young Adults," we have explored a variety of important subjects related to personal finance, including investing techniques, the fundamentals of budgeting, and the concept of financial independence. As we come to an end, let's go over some important lessons learned and stress the need to put financial methods into practice. After all, you too can achieve financial freedom!

Important lessons learned

1. Financial Literacy Matters: Having a solid understanding of personal finance principles enables you to manage your money wisely, make wise decisions, and accumulate savings for the future.

2. Budgeting is Fundamental: Setting up a budget enables you to prioritize your spending, keep tabs on your earnings and outlays, and make progress toward your financial objectives.

3. Investing and Savings: Making prudent investments and setting aside money for long-term and emergency goals are crucial to accumulating wealth and ensuring financial security.

4. Debt Management: Retaining good financial health depends on avoiding the debt trap, comprehending credit scores, and managing debt sensibly.

5. Career and Income Growth: The first stages to achieving financial security and career progress are selecting a work path that fits your interests and objectives, haggling over pay and perks, and making long-term career plans.

6. Real-World Scenarios: Managing real-world financial scenarios calls for preparation, knowledge, and well-informed decision-making. These could range from renting to buying a property to

understanding insurance and getting ready for life events.

7. Building Wealth: Long-term financial objectives can be met by investing in assets, producing passive income, and adopting the concepts of financial independence.

8. Giving Back: Contributing to your community, supporting causes you care about, and striking a balance between personal wealth and social duty are all essential components of wealth stewardship and leaving a lasting legacy.

Motivation

Remember that every little step you take toward financial empowerment and literacy will help you get closer to your goals as you set out on your financial path. Every step you take now, whether it's making a budget, opening a savings account, beginning to invest, or exploring opportunities for passive income, adds up to a better financial future.

Attaining financial freedom is not merely an aspirational goal; it is attainable through dedication, perseverance, and a readiness to adapt and develop. Take charge of your finances, accumulate wealth, and design the life you want by putting the techniques and ideas covered in this book into practice.

So, do not delay any longer. Start right now. Take the first step toward financial empowerment and keep in mind that you can achieve financial freedom and live a prosperous, abundant life with hard work and dedication.

Conclusion

In summary, "Smart Money Moves" has given you the information and resources you need to successfully and confidently traverse the realm of personal finance. Remember that achieving financial freedom is not just a pipe dream; rather, it is something you can attain with dedication and hard work. Now is the time to act and start on the path to prosperity and financial empowerment.

AFTERWORD

As you reach the conclusion of "Smart Money Moves: A Guide for Teens and Young Adults," I want to extend my heartfelt congratulations on taking this important step towards financial literacy and empowerment. Whether you've just begun your journey or you've already started implementing some of the strategies outlined in this book, know that you've already taken a significant leap towards securing your financial future.

As you reflect on the principles and insights shared within these pages, remember that financial literacy is not just about numbers and calculationsâ€"it's about mindset and empowerment. By adopting a proactive approach to managing your money, you're not only setting yourself up for financial success, but you're also cultivating a mindset of responsibility, resilience, and resourcefulness that will serve you well in all areas of your life.

But the journey towards financial independence is not without its challenges. Along the way, you may encounter setbacks, unexpected expenses, or moments of doubt. In those moments, remember the lessons you've learned from "Smart Money Moves" and draw upon the knowledge and skills you've acquired to overcome obstacles and stay on track towards your goals.

And remember, you're not alone on this journey. Seek out mentors, advisors, and peers who can offer guidance, support, and encouragement along the way. Share your successes and challenges with others, and celebrate each milestone you achieve on your path to financial freedom.

Finally, I want to thank you for investing your time and energy into your financial education. By prioritizing your financial well-being today, you're laying the groundwork for a brighter and more prosperous future tomorrow. Keep learning, keep growing, and never underestimate the power of smart money moves to transform your life for the better.

Wishing you all the success and prosperity in the world,

Kuphrey Eshiet

ACKNOWLEDGEMENT

I would like to express my deepest gratitude to all those who have contributed to the creation of "Smart Money Moves: A Guide for Teens and Young Adults."

First and foremost, I extend my heartfelt thanks to my family for their unwavering support and encouragement throughout this journey. Your belief in me has been a constant source of strength and inspiration.

I am incredibly grateful to my mentors and advisors, whose guidance and wisdom have shaped my understanding of personal finance and helped me distill complex concepts into accessible and actionable insights.

To my friends and colleagues who provided valuable feedback and encouragement along the way, thank you for your support and camaraderie.

A special thank you to the readers and supporters of "Smart Money Moves." Your enthusiasm for financial education fuels my passion for empowering young people to take control of their financial futures.

I would also like to acknowledge the countless authors, educators, and experts whose work has informed and inspired the content of this book. Your contributions to the field of personal finance have paved the way for a new generation of financially literate individuals.

To all those who have played a part in this endeavor, thank you from the bottom of my heart.

With gratitude,

Kuphrey

ABOUT THE AUTHOR

Kuphrey Eshiet

Kuphrey Eshiet, the creator of "Smart Money Moves: A Guide for Teens and Young Adults," is a passionate advocate for financial literacy and empowerment. With a background in Economics, Kuphrey has dedicated his career to helping young people gain the knowledge and skills they need to succeed in the world of personal finance.

Through his work Kuphrey is empowering countless individuals to take control of their financial futures, offering practical advice and actionable strategies for building wealth and achieving financial independence.

With a clear and engaging writing style, Kuphrey distills complex financial concepts into accessible and easy-to-understand language, making "Smart Money Moves" a must-read for anyone looking to master the fundamentals of money management.

Outside of his writing and advocacy work, Kuphrey enjoys speaking., entrepreneurship, etc. and is committed to lifelong learning and personal growth.

Through his dedication to financial education and empowerment, Kuphrey Eshiet continues to inspire and empower young people to make smart financial decisions and build a brighter future for themselves.

"Financial freedom is not merely the destination, but the empowering journey of mastering your money and shaping your destiny."